# REPTILES AND AMPHIBIANS

Written by Mary Scott
Illustrated by Janice Kinnealy

**Troll Associates**

# COPPERHEAD

Snakes are reptiles. All reptiles are *cold-blooded*—their bodies are the same temperature as the air around them. Reptiles also have dry, scaly skin. Most reptiles live on land.

A copperhead has 2 special teeth, called *fangs*. They are filled with a poison called *venom*. A copperhead's bite can make a person very sick. And it can kill mice, rats, and other small animals, which this snake likes to eat.

*Library of Congress Cataloging-in-Publication Data*

Scott, Mary, (date)
    A picture book of reptiles and amphibians / by Mary Scott;
illustrated by Janice Kinnealy.
        p.    cm.
    Summary: Describes the physical characteristics and behavior of a
variety of reptiles and amphibians, including the cricket frog,
copperhead, and snapping turtle.
    ISBN 0-8167-2838-0 (lib. bdg.)        ISBN 0-8167-2839-9 (pbk.)
    1. Reptiles—Juvenile literature.   2. Amphibians—Juvenile
literature.  [1. Reptiles.   2. Amphibians.]   I. Kinnealy, Janice,
ill.  II. Title.
QL644.2.S36   1993
597.9—dc20
                                                        92-19054

# HORNED LIZARD

The spikes on its head give this strange-looking lizard its name. It is also sometimes called a *horned toad*, because its body is shaped a little like a toad's. The horned lizard is part of the reptile family.

Horned lizards live in deserts and other dry areas. If danger is near, this lizard can dig itself into the sand and quickly disappear. It can also scare its enemies by squirting blood from the corners of its eyes!

# LEOPARD FROG

Frogs are part of a group called *amphibians* (am-FIB-ee-uns). An amphibian spends the first part of its life in the water. Later, its body changes and it lives on land.

A leopard frog is about 3 inches (7.6 centimeters) long. Like all frogs, its back legs are very long and strong. This helps the frog swim quickly. A frog's back legs also make it a great jumper. Many frogs can jump 5 to 10 feet (1½ to 3 meters) in one hop. That's a long trip for a little frog!

# TADPOLE

Most frogs lay their eggs in the water. Some lay several thousand eggs at a time! After a few days or weeks, the eggs hatch into tiny tadpoles. A tadpole has a tail and no legs. It breathes through gills, just like a fish does, and lives in the water.

In time, a tadpole's body begins to change. It grows legs. Lungs develop, and the gills disappear. Now the tadpole is a frog, and it can live on land. This change from tadpole to frog is called *metamorphosis* (met-ah-MORE-fo-sis).

CROCODILE

ALLIGATOR

6

# CROCODILE

How can you tell a crocodile and an alligator apart? They are both reptiles, but a crocodile's jaw is pointed. An alligator's is rounded. And some of a crocodile's teeth stick out when its mouth is closed. An alligator's teeth all fit in its closed jaws.

Like most reptiles, crocodiles lay eggs. The mother buries her eggs so they will be warm and safe. She digs them out when the babies are ready to hatch.

# ALLIGATOR

Alligators are heavier than crocodiles. They live in fresh water, and like to eat fish, turtles, crabs, and birds. Male alligators are bigger than females. They can weigh up to 550 pounds (249 kilograms) and be up to 12 feet (3.7 meters) long.

An alligator uses its short legs to walk on land. In the water, it swims by moving its tail from side to side.

# GARTER SNAKE

Most snakes lay eggs. But the garter snake gives birth to live young. A garter snake can have 20 or more babies at a time. Even though the snakes are only a few inches (centimeters) long when they are born, they can find food and take care of themselves right away.

Garter snakes are not poisonous. This is a good thing, because this snake is very common in parks, gardens, and backyards all over North America.

# MUDPUPPY

The mudpuppy is
a type of amphibian
called a *salamander*
(SAL-uh-man-der).
Most amphibians
live in water until their bodies change and they
can live on land. But mudpuppies spend their
whole lives in the water. They usually hide in
the plants at the bottom of ponds or lakes.
They eat worms, fish eggs, crayfish, and other
water animals. When a mudpuppy is
frightened, it makes a barking noise.
That is how this animal got its
name.

# CRICKET FROG

Cricket frogs got their name because they make a sound like a cricket's chirp. These frogs are very small—only about ¾ to 1½ inches (1.9 to 3.8 centimeters) long. They are one of the smallest frogs.

# BULLFROG

The bullfrog is the largest frog in North America. Its body can be up to 8 inches (20 centimeters) long and its legs can add another 10 inches (25 centimeters).

Bullfrogs live near ponds or slow-moving streams. They sit in the water or on the shore, watching for insects. When one flies by, the frog catches it by flicking out its long, sticky tongue. Bullfrogs also eat worms, spiders, other frogs, and many other small animals.

# KOMODO DRAGON

This reptile is the largest lizard alive today. It can measure up to 10 feet (3 meters) long, and weighs up to 350 pounds (160 kilograms).

Komodo (kuh-MOH-doh) dragons are found on islands in Indonesia, in southeast Asia. Even though it has a large, heavy body, the dragon can move very quickly. It is strong enough to kill small deer and wild pigs, as well as smaller animals. Its sharp teeth, long claws, and heavy tail make good weapons.

# PAINTED SALAMANDER

Salamanders look a lot like lizards, but they are actually part of the amphibian family. Most salamanders live on land, but they like damp places. Underneath a rock or a log is a favorite spot. Painted salamanders live in the western part of North America. They are about 5 inches (12.7 centimeters) long and brightly colored.

# SPOTTED SALAMANDER

The spotted salamander lays its eggs in ponds. The young, or *larvae* (LAR-vee), have gills and live in the water. But when they get older, their bodies change. Then the salamanders live on land.

The spotted salamander lives in moist woods. It eats worms and insects by catching them on its sticky tongue.

# SNAPPING TURTLE

Turtles are part of the reptile family. They are the only reptiles that have a shell. Most turtles can pull their legs, head, and tail inside the shell for protection. The snapping turtle has a long neck and very strong jaws. It usually lies in the mud at the bottom of lakes, and eats fish, frogs, insects, small birds, and other animals. If you find a snapping turtle, it's best not to touch it. It may take a bite out of you!

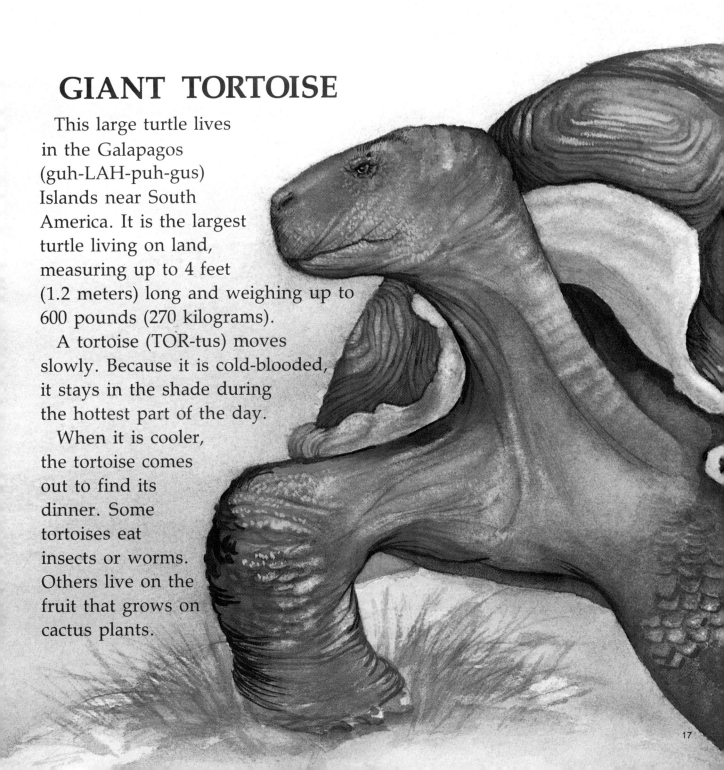

# GIANT TORTOISE

This large turtle lives in the Galapagos (guh-LAH-puh-gus) Islands near South America. It is the largest turtle living on land, measuring up to 4 feet (1.2 meters) long and weighing up to 600 pounds (270 kilograms).

A tortoise (TOR-tus) moves slowly. Because it is cold-blooded, it stays in the shade during the hottest part of the day.

When it is cooler, the tortoise comes out to find its dinner. Some tortoises eat insects or worms. Others live on the fruit that grows on cactus plants.

# COMMON TOAD

Toads and frogs are both amphibians. They look alike, but there are a few ways to tell them apart. A toad's skin is dry and bumpy, while a frog has damp, smooth skin. Toads are also heavier and slower than frogs, and spend more time on land than frogs do.

American toads live in gardens and woods. They do not like the heat. To keep cool, they will bury themselves in the mud. They usually come out at night to hunt for insects.

# FOWLER'S TOAD

Toads have several ways to protect themselves from animals that like to eat them. They can hide in a hole, or play dead. Sometimes they puff up their bodies to look bigger and scarier. A toad also has a pair of glands on top of its head. These glands release a bad-tasting poison that can make other animals sick.

The fowler's toad lives in North America. It eats insects by catching them on its tongue.

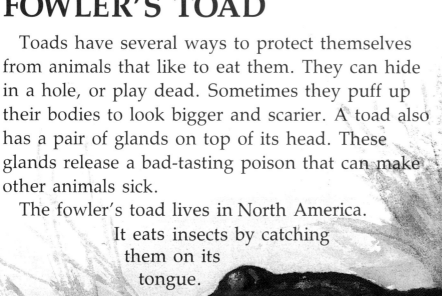

# GILA MONSTER

The Gila (HEE-lah) monster is a lizard. It lives in the deserts of the southwestern United States and Mexico. This poisonous reptile spends the hottest part of the day underground or in the shade of a rock. At night it comes out to hunt mice and other lizards, or steal bird and reptile eggs out of their nests. A gila monster stores fat in its tail. It can live on this fat for several months.

# SPINY IGUANA

The iguana (ig-WAH-nuh) is a reptile that lives in deserts and other dry areas. You aren't likely to see an iguana in the wild, but they are often sold in pet stores.

Spiny iguanas are about 1 to 4 feet (.3 to 1.2 meters) long. They eat fruit, leaves, and flowers. When a female iguana is ready to lay her eggs, she digs a tunnel and buries up to 75 eggs there. About 2 weeks later, the baby iguanas hatch and dig their way to the surface. Young iguanas take up to 2 years to reach adult size. But they can take care of themselves as soon as they are born.

# SCARLET KING SNAKE

This colorful snake is not poisonous, but it looks a lot like the poisonous coral snake. This fools enemies and scares them away.

The scarlet king snake eats mice and other small animals. It kills animals by constriction (con-STRIK-shun). The snake wraps the coils of its body around an animal and squeezes. The animal soon dies because it cannot breathe. Then the snake stretches its jaws wide and swallows its dinner whole.

# CORAL SNAKE

The coral snake lives in the southern United States. It usually lies in a damp, cool spot under fallen leaves, and looks for lizards or other snakes to eat.

Coral snakes are very poisonous. The bright stripes on its body warn people and animals to stay away from this dangerous snake.

**Newt**

# INDEX